A LIFEGUIDE BIBLE STUDY

JOSHUA

The Power of God's Promises

12 Studies
for individuals or groups

Donald Baker

With Notes for Leaders

INTERVARSITY PRESS
DOWNERS GROVE, ILLINOIS 60515

InterVarsity Press® is the book-publishing division of InterVarsity Christian Fellowship®, a student movement active on campus at hundreds of universities, colleges and schools of nursing in the United States of America, and a member movement of the International Fellowship of Evangelical Students. For information about local and regional activities, write Public Relations Dept., InterVarsity Christian Fellowship, 6400 Schroeder Rd., P.O. Box 7895, Madison, WI 53707-7895.

LifeGuide® is a registered trademark of InterVarsity Christian Fellowship.

Cover photograph: Peter French

ISBN 0-8308-1024-2

Contents

Getting the Most
from LifeGuide Bible Studies

Many of us long to fill our minds and our lives with Scripture. We desire to be transformed by its message. LifeGuide Bible Studies are designed to be an exciting and challenging way to do just that. They help us to be guided by God's Word in every area of life.

How They Work

LifeGuides have a number of distinctive features. Perhaps the most important is that they are *inductive* rather than *deductive*. In other words, they lead us to *discover* what the Bible says rather than simply *telling* us what it says.

They are also thought provoking. They help us to think about the meaning of the passage so that we can truly understand what the author is saying. The questions require more than one-word answers.

The studies are personal. Questions expose us to the promises, assurances, exhortations and challenges of God's Word. They are designed to allow the Scriptures to renew our minds so that we can be transformed by the Spirit of God. This is the ultimate goal of all Bible study.

The studies are versatile. They are designed for student, neighborhood and church groups. They are also effective for individual study.

How They're Put Together

LifeGuides also have a distinctive format. Each study need take no more than forty-five minutes in a group setting or thirty minutes in personal study—unless you choose to take more time.

The studies can be used within a quarter system in a church and fit well in a semester or trimester system on a college campus. If a guide has more than thirteen studies, it is divided into two or occasionally three parts of approximately twelve studies each.

LifeGuides use a workbook format. Space is provided for writing answers to each question. This is ideal for personal study and allows group members to prepare in advance for the discussion.

The studies also contain leader's notes. They show how to lead a group discussion, provide additional background information on certain questions, give helpful tips on group dynamics and suggest ways to deal with problems which may arise during the discussion. With such helps, someone with little or no experience can lead an effective study.

Suggestions for Individual Study

1. As you begin each study, pray that God will help you to understand and apply the passage to your life.

2. Read and reread the assigned Bible passage to familiarize yourself with what the author is saying. In the case of book studies, you may want to read through the entire book prior to the first study. This will give you a helpful overview of its contents.

3. A good modern translation of the Bible, rather than the King James Version or a paraphrase, will give you the most help. The New International Version, the New American Standard Bible and the Revised Standard Version are all recommended. However, the questions in this guide are based on the New International Version.

4. Write your answers in the space provided in the study guide. This will help you to express your understanding of the passage clearly.

5. It might be good to have a Bible dictionary handy. Use it to look up any unfamiliar words, names or places.

Suggestions for Group Study

1. Come to the study prepared. Follow the suggestions for individual study mentioned above. You will find that careful preparation will greatly enrich your time spent in group discussion.

2. Be willing to participate in the discussion. The leader of your group will not be lecturing. Instead, he or she will be encouraging the members of the group to discuss what they have learned from the passage. The leader will be asking the questions that are found in this guide. Plan to share what God has taught you in your individual study.

3. Stick to the passage being studied. Your answers should be based on the verses which are the focus of the discussion and not on outside authorities such as commentaries or speakers. This guide deliberately avoids jumping

from book to book or passage to passage. Each study focuses on only one passage. Book studies are generally designed to lead you through the book in the order in which it was written. This will help you follow the author's argument.

4. Be sensitive to the other members of the group. Listen attentively when they share what they have learned. You may be surprised by their insights! Link what you say to the comments of others so the group stays on the topic. Also, be affirming whenever you can. This will encourage some of the more hesitant members of the group to participate.

5. Be careful not to dominate the discussion. We are sometimes so eager to share what we have learned that we leave too little opportunity for others to respond. By all means participate! But allow others to also.

6. Expect God to teach you through the passage being discussed and through the other members of the group. Pray that you will have an enjoyable and profitable time together.

7. If you are the discussion leader, you will find additional suggestions and helpful ideas for each study in the leader's notes. These are found at the back of the guide.

Introducing Joshua

Can we count on God to keep his promises?

Thousands of years ago God promised Abraham, "I will make you a great nation" (Gen 12:2). "To your descendants I give this land, from the river of Egypt to the great river, the Euphrates" (Gen 15:18). These same promises were renewed with each generation of Abraham's descendants, but hundreds of years passed and his children still had no land to call their own. Even worse, they lived as slaves for four hundred years and wandered in the desert forty years after that. They hardly qualified as a great nation!

The book of Joshua is the story of God making good on his promises. It tells how Israel entered and conquered the land God had promised them. In fact, God's faithfulness is so complete that at the end of the book we hear this proclamation: "You know with all your heart and soul that not one of all the good promises the LORD your God gave you has failed. Every promise has been fulfilled; not one has failed" (Josh 23:14).

Can we count on God to keep his promises? The answer from Joshua is a resounding "Yes!" God is utterly dependable, and we can trust him completly. Joshua is a book for those whose prayers seem to go unanswered, for those who wonder if God is really alive and active, and for those who desire fresh assurance of God's dependability.

Joshua is also a fast-paced book. In it we share the excitement of the Israelites, who through God's power saw a river dry up and a city wall tumble. We watch them face overwhelming odds and emerge victorious.

The book of Joshua picks up the story of Israel's history after the death of Moses and carries it through the entry, conquest and division of the Promised Land. The events recorded began around 1406 B.C. and ended about twenty-four years later.

Although the author of the book is not identified, the traditional view is that it was written by Joshua himself, with a few additions made by Eleazar or Phinehas (for example, the reference to Joshua's death in 24:29-30). However, some scholars believe that the book may have been written by a younger contemporary of Joshua, and still others think it was not written until the beginning of the monarchy by someone who had access to various records of the actual events.

This guide will take you through Joshua in twelve studies. Each study focuses on God's faithfulness and what we can learn from Israel's example as they enter and conquer the Promised Land. May you be challenged and encouraged by this action-filled book!

1
Get Ready to Go

Joshua 1

Ｇod sometimes asks us to do things that seem far beyond our abilities. He might ask us to assume a position of leadership, or take on a demanding project or begin a Bible study with our non-Christian friends. At such times it is easy to feel underqualified and overwhelmed.

Imagine trying to fill the shoes of someone as legendary as Moses! This was the task Joshua faced. You will notice that the name Moses pops up many times in the book of Joshua. At times Joshua must have felt that the memory of Moses hung over him like a dark cloud. Now that it was his turn to lead, Joshua needed to know if the people would follow him as they had Moses. More importantly, he needed to know if God intended to help him as he had Moses.

1. How do you react when faced with something you feel totally unqualified to do?

2. Read Joshua 1. What emotions might Joshua be feeling as he takes command of the Israelites and prepares to cross the Jordan?

3. What promises does the Lord make to Joshua (vv. 1-9)?

How would these promises strengthen and encourage him?

4. The promise "I will never leave you nor forsake you" (v. 5) is also quoted in the New Testament (Heb 13:5). How can this promise strengthen and encourage us in the midst of life's challenges?

5. What commands does the Lord give to Joshua (vv. 6-9)?

6. What is the relationship between God's promises and his commands?

7. How can meditating on Scripture and being careful to do what it says enable us to be prosperous and successful (see Ps 1:1-3)?

8. Why is Joshua especially concerned about the tribes of Reuben, Gad and Manasseh (vv. 12-15; see Num 32:1-27)?

9. How is God's presence made evident in the response he receives from the tribes (vv. 16-18)?

10. What challenging task do you face in the near future?

11. Thank God for his presence and strength as you seek to obey him in that situation.

2
Rahab's Life-Changing Faith

Joshua 2

How can we recognize genuine faith? What does it look like? How does it act?

In this study we meet a woman of faith, a member of the only family in Jericho whom God allowed Israel to spare. Because of Rahab's faith, not only was her life spared but God extended to her the promises he had made to Israel. She became an ancestor of both King David and Jesus. She is mentioned in James as an example of saving faith. She is also honored in Hebrews 11, "The Faith Hall of Fame." Not bad for someone known throughout history as "Rahab the prostitute"!

1. Think of someone you would describe as a person of strong faith. How has that person's faith affected his or her daily life?

2. Read Joshua 2. What risks does Rahab take in protecting the spies (vv. 1-7)?

3. What does Rahab know and believe about the God of Israel (vv. 8-11)?

4. How is her risk-taking related to her faith?

5. What risks does your faith require you to take?

6. What deal does Rahab make in exchange for helping the spies (vv. 12-16)?

7. What conditions must she and her family fulfill in order to be saved (vv. 17-21)?

8. How are these conditions similar to those of the first Passover, when Israel was redeemed from Egypt (see Ex 12:21-23)?

9. A missionary named Jim Elliot once made the statement, "He is no fool who gives what he cannot keep to gain what he cannot lose." How might this statement apply to Rahab?

10. Look back over the chapter and summarize all the actions Rahab took because of her faith.

11. Why must a genuine faith express itself in actions?

12. What actions have you taken recently as a direct result of your faith in Christ?

13. What effect did Rahab's faith have on the Israelites (vv. 22-24)?

14. How can our faith have a positive effect on both Christians and non-Christians?

3
Crossing the Jordan

Joshua 3:1 — 5:12

God's blessings are given for a purpose. He wants us to grow in our love for him as we experience kindness upon kindness. These chapters contain several reminders of all God did in leading Israel from Egypt to the Promised Land. They teach us the importance of remembering and celebrating what God has done for us.

1. In what ways are we reminded of significant people or events in our nation's history?

2. Read Joshua 3. Imagine life with the Israelites during their three days of encampment along the Jordan. What thoughts and conversations do you expect they had?

3. The Israelites consecrated themselves (v. 5) by washing their garments and by abstaining from sexual intercourse (see Ex 19:10, 14-15). Why would it have been important for them to consecrate themselves at this time?

4. How and when should we consecrate ourselves?

5. Describe the sequence of events the Israelites would have seen as they crossed the Jordan (vv. 3-4, 8-17)?

What do you think they thought and felt during the crossing?

6. Read Joshua 4. Why was this miraculous crossing especially important for Joshua's leadership (3:7 and 4:14)?

7. What other goals did this miracle accomplish (3:10; 4:24; see 5:1)?

8. How would the twelve stones from the Jordan River serve as a memorial for future generations (4:1-7, 19-24)?

9. What memorials do you have to remind yourself and future generations of what God has done?

10. Read Joshua 5:1-12. Circumcision was the sign of the covenant between God and Israel. Why was it important for the Israelites to be circumcised at this time?

11. The first Passover had been celebrated forty years earlier, on the day of Israel's deliverance from Egypt (Ex 12). What significance would the Passover have for those who had just crossed the Jordan and entered the Promised Land (v. 10)?

12. In what ways are circumcision and the Passover similar to today's celebrations of baptism and the Lord's Supper?

13. What have these chapters taught you about remembering and celebrating the things God has done?

4
Jericho Falls

Joshua 5:13—6:27

We fight many battles in life—financial, physical, emotional and spiritual. How can we be victorious in these struggles, especially when the odds against us seem overwhelming?

Conquering the Promised Land was an enormous task. Forty years earlier the Israelites had lamented, "The land we explored devours those living in it. All the people we saw there are of great size. . . . We seemed like grasshoppers in our own eyes, and we looked the same to them" (Num 13:32-33). Yet in spite of these obstacles, Joshua and the people of Israel now set out to conquer the first Canaanite stronghold—Jericho. As they do so, the Lord teaches them and us how to be victorious.

---

1. When have you felt that God was fighting your battles for you?

What was your part in that experience?

---

2. Read Joshua 5:13—6:27. How do you think the visit by the commander of the army of the Lord affected Joshua (vv. 13-15)?

3. When Joshua asked the commander of the Lord's army, "Are you for us or for our enemies?" he replied, "Neither" (v. 14). What is the difference between the Lord joining our side and our joining the Lord's side?

4. In what ways do the Lord's instructions for the conquest of Jericho seem strange (6:1-5)?

5. What was the significance of carrying the ark of the covenant and blowing the trumpets?

6. How do you think the Israelites felt during this seven-day spectacle (vv. 6-16)?

What impact do you think it had on the inhabitants of Jericho?

7. What lessons was God teaching the Israelites during their seven days of marching?

8. How is our spiritual warfare today similar to and different from Israel's conquest of Jericho (see 2 Cor 10:3-5)?

9. What did it mean for this city and its contents to be devoted to the Lord (6:17-25)?

10. Why didn't God allow the Israelites to keep any of the spoils of war?

What does this teach about the things we "earn"?

11. What spiritual battles are you currently fighting?

12. What principles of victory have you learned from Israel's conquest of Jericho?

5
Defeat, Confession and Victory

Joshua 7—8

Success can lead to complacency. We feel confident, in control, optimistic—then suddenly the bottom drops out of our lives.

Israel had tasted success. They had entered the Promised Land, they had won an important battle, and God was obviously with them. Conquering the city of Ai would be a piece of cake! But their confidence collapsed when they attacked the city and were routed. What had gone wrong? Had God failed them? Why hadn't God kept his promise?

1. Think of a time when you failed at something. How did you feel, and why?

2. Read Joshua 7. Imagine trudging back to camp with the defeated Israelites (vv. 1-5). What would have been going through your mind?

3. What are Joshua's concerns after this defeat (vv. 6-9)?

4. How do God's concerns differ from Joshua's (vv. 10-15)?

5. If you had been Achan, how would you have felt as your tribe, your clan, your family, and finally you yourself were presented before God (vv. 14-22)?

6. Why don't most of us experience a similar horror over the realization of our own sins?

7. Joshua urged Achan to "give glory to the LORD" by admitting his crime (v. 19). How does confession glorify God?

8. Joshua stated that Achan was being stoned because he had brought disaster on the Israelites (v. 25). Thirty-six Israelite warriors had already died because of Achan's sin. How might our sins affect others?

9. Read Joshua 8. How did the second attack on Ai differ from the first (vv. 1-29)?

What was the Lord's involvement in each of the two battles?

---

10. If you had been an Israelite, what thoughts would have come to mind each time you saw the rock piles mentioned in 7:26 and 8:29?

---

11. Why did Joshua build the altar on Mount Ebal (vv. 30-31)?

---

12. What impact would the reading of the law have had on the Israelites (vv. 32-35)?

---

13. What reminders can help keep us from sinning?

6
Deceived

Joshua 9

Satan's primary strategy is deceit. He seduces us into believing that a lie is truth, that evil is good and that a "suicidal plunge is really a leap into life."*

In the previous study, Israel moved from victory to defeat and back to victory. On that occasion the defeat was caused by the deliberate disobedience of one man. In this study Israel suffers another setback, but this time their disobedience is not deliberate—they are deceived.

1. How do you decide whether to make a decision on your own or to pray about it first?

2. Read Joshua 9. When they hear about Israel's victories, how does the Gibeonites' reaction differ from that of the kings west of the Jordan (vv. 1-6)?

3. What made the Gibeonite deception so convincing to the Israelites (vv. 7-13)?

4. The Israelites were fooled because they "did not inquire of the LORD" (v. 14). Why should they have known that this was not a decision to be made on their own?

5. What tricks does Satan use to keep us from seeking God's guidance?

6. The Gibeonites are similar to Rahab in that, for both, their faith led them to lie. Why aren't the Gibeonites commended for their faith as Rahab was?

7. What do we learn from this about faith?

8. What did the Israelites known about making peace with distant and neighboring cities (Deut 20:10-18)?

9. Why did the Israelites take their oath so seriously, even though it was based on a lie (vv. 16-19)?

10. The danger in sparing the Gibeonites was that they might entice Israel to idolatry and other pagan practices (Deut 20:18). How would Joshua's curse on them have helped to solve the problem?

11. In what areas are we tempted to make peace with a sinful world?

12. How can we guard ourselves against these deceptive alliances?

---

*Derek Kidner, *Genesis* (Downers Grove, Ill.: InterVarsity Press, 1967), p. 68.

7
The Lord Fights for Israel

Joshua 10—12

God demonstrates his faithfulness to every Christian. He strengthens us when we are weak, comforts us when we are suffering, heals us when we are sick. He provides for all of our physical, emotional and spiritual needs. After all this, why do we often find it difficult to trust him?

Joshua and Israel had miraculously crossed the Jordan and conquered the cities of Jericho and Ai. Yet in spite of these victories, they still needed to be reassured that God was with them.

1. Why is it often hard to trust God for the future even though he has been faithful in the past?

2. Read Joshua 10. What do you imagine the Amorites and the Gibeonites were feeling as they prepared to battle each other (vv. 1-6)?

3. The Lord tells Joshua, "Do not be afraid of them; I have given them into your hand" (v. 8). After miraculously crossing the Jordan and conquering Jericho and Ai, why would Joshua need this reassurance?

4. In spite of past victories, in what areas do you need to be reassured of God's presence and power? Explain.

5. Verse 14 concludes, "Surely the LORD was fighting for Israel!" How is this obvious from verses 9-15?

6. How would these events have provided the encouragement Joshua needed?

7. After the Lord reassures him, how does Joshua reassure his army about future battles (vv. 16-27)?

8. What can we do to encourage others about God's faithfulness?

9. How does the Lord demonstrate his faithfulness to Israel during the southern campaign (vv. 29-43)?

10. Read Joshua 11—12. After the stunning victories in the south, a new and more powerful force aligns itself against Israel (11:1-5). What thoughts do you imagine went through Joshua's mind as he received reports of this new alliance?

11. During the northern campaign, how does Joshua demonstrate his obedience to the Lord (vv. 6-23)?

12. Why is our obedience an important factor if we wish to see God's power?

13. In chapters 11—12 we do not read of any miraculous intervention by God as we did in previous chapters. How did the Israelites know that God was still the one giving them the victory?

14. How can we know that God is still with us even when we don't see a miracle?

8
Joshua Divides the Land

Joshua 13–19

Christians often feel more like captives than conquerors. What hinders our spiritual progress? Why do we sometimes experience so little when we are promised so much?

God had proven himself to Israel throughout their many battles. He had promised to be with them in the conquest of Canaan and had kept his promise. Yet in spite of many victories, much of the land remained to be conquered. These chapters look at why Israel had failed to possess all that God had promised.

1. In what one area of your life would you most like to see spiritual progress?

2. Read Joshua 13:1-7. The Lord commands Joshua to divide the land even though much of it remains to be conquered. What does that command—and Joshua's willingness to obey it—reveal about the Lord and about Joshua?

3. Read Joshua 14:6-15. How is Caleb's faith just as strong at eighty-five as it had been at forty?

4. Read Joshua 15:63, 16:10, 17:12-13 and 19:47. God had promised to drive these Canaanites out of the land. Why then do you think Israel had difficulty dislodging them (see also Ex 23:29-30 and Deut 7:22-24)?

5. Read Joshua 17:14-18. How does the attitude of the people of Joseph contrast with that of Caleb?

6. How does Joshua deal with their complaint?

7. We sometimes act like the people of Joseph, complaining about how little God has given us when we have not fully used what we have. How do you think Joshua would respond to our complaints and excuses?

8. Read Joshua 18:1-10. Seven tribes had not yet received their inheritance. What was their problem?

9. How does Joshua help them to make a fair distribution of the land?

10. As you look back over these chapters, what reasons can you give for why Israel had difficulty taking full possession of the land?

11. Which reasons help to explain why God's promises to us are sometimes only partially fulfilled? (For example, his promise to purify our lives of sin.) Explain.

12. Does your response to God's promises more closely resemble that of:
a. Caleb (wholehearted faith and obedience)?
b. the tribes of Manasseh and Ephraim (disobedience)?
c. the people of Joseph (complaints, lack of faith)?
d. the seven tribes (procrastination)?
Explain your answer.

13. What can you do to become more like Caleb?

9
The Lord Fulfills His Promises

Joshua 20—21

How does faith differ from wishful thinking? Why should we expect God to answer our prayers, to provide us with food and clothing or to be involved in jobs or family? How do we know our faith isn't simply foolishness?

Scripture tells us that true faith must be grounded in God's promises. If God has promised to do something, then we can trust him wholeheartedly. If he has not promised to do something, then all the faith in the world won't make it happen. In Joshua 20—21 we see the final outcome of God's promises to Israel.

1. Think of a time recently when you trusted God for something. Which of his promises applied to that situation?

2. Read Joshua 20. What was the purpose of the cities of refuge?

3. The cities of refuge were all inhabited by Levites, the tribe responsible for the priesthood and temple service. Why would their cities be well-suited as places of refuge?

4. What does the command to establish these cities teach us about the Lord?

5. Quickly skim Joshua 21:1-42. How did the Levites differ from the other tribes (see Josh 13:14, 33; 14:3-4; 18:7)?

6. How did God provide for their needs?

7. What do you think God's purpose was in scattering the Levites throughout the land?

8. What principles for missions and ministry can we draw from God's plans for the Levites?

9. Read Joshua 21:43-45. How do these verses provide the climax to the book of Joshua?

10. Verse 45 states, "Not one of all the LORD's good promises to the house of Israel failed; every one was fulfilled." As you think back over the book of Joshua, what specific examples of God's faithfulness can you recall?

11. What are some of the promises God has made to us as Christians?

12. In what ways have you seen God fulfill these promises in your life?

10
Will the Nation Survive?

Joshua 22

T he tribes which had been given land on the east side of the Jordan had fulfilled their commitment to the rest of Israel. They had entered the Promised Land with the others and had helped them to fight. Now it was time for them to return to their own homes. But since the Israelites would be living on both sides of the river, the Jordan Rift Valley became a natural barrier which hindered the unity of the twelve tribes. Could Israel still remain unified? Their response to a national crisis illustrates principles for maintaining Christian unity.

1. What are some of the barriers to true Christian unity?

2. Read Joshua 22. Why does Joshua commend the tribes of Reuben, Gad and Manasseh (vv. 1-4)?

3. Why would Joshua feel it was important to remind these tribes to obey God's law (v. 5)?

4. What blessings had these tribes received from God because of their faithful service (vv. 6-9)?

5. How does God reward us for faithful service?

6. Why were the western tribes prepared to do battle over the issue of the altar (vv. 10-20; see also Deut 12:1-14)?

7. Phinehas reminds the eastern tribes of the plagues brought on by the worship of Peor (see Num 25) and the sin of Achan (see Josh 7). How did he think those situations applied to the present one?

8. What reasons did the eastern tribes have for building the altar (vv. 21-29)?

9. How did both sides in this dispute show that they were honoring God?

10. What can we learn from this story about confronting those whose actions seem offensive?

11. What should our attitude be toward those who have misunderstood our actions?

12. What principles do you find in this chapter for restoring and maintaining unity in your church or fellowship group?

11
Joshua's Farewell

Joshua 23

Great leaders inspire us to obey God. We depend on their encouragement and their example. But what happens when such leaders are no longer around?

About twenty years elapsed between the end of the war and Joshua's death. During that time, Joshua's influence kept Israel loyal to God. Now Joshua knows that he is about to die, and he is concerned that Israel's loyalty to God might not continue in his absence. Therefore, he calls the Israelites together to hear a farewell message of challenge and warning.

1. If you were giving a farewell address, what would you most want to say?

2. Read Joshua 23. How does Joshua exalt God in his farewell address?

3. Why is it important for us to recall the Lord's faithfulness in past events?

4. In what past events have you been struck by God's faithfulness?

5. What promises and commands does Joshua give to Israel (vv. 5-11)?

6. What does it mean for us to "hold fast to the LORD" and "to love the LORD" (vv. 8, 11)?

7. Why weren't the Israelites allowed to associate with the nations around them (vv. 7-8, 12-13)?

8. Today, what aspects of non-Christian culture can become snares, traps, whips on our backs and thorns in our eyes?

9. We obviously cannot and should not avoid non-Christians today. How then can we resist the temptation to live like them?

10. Joshua warns that the Lord is not only faithful to his promises but also to his threats (vv. 14-16). What threats had the Lord made to Israel (vv. 15-16)?

11. What warnings has the Lord given us as Christians (Acts 20:28-31; Gal 5:19-21; Eph 5:3-7; Heb 2:1-4)?

12. How does Joshua's farewell address motivate you to be faithful to the Lord?

12
Who Will Serve the Lord?

Joshua 24

Throughout the book of Joshua, the Lord has demonstrated his faithfulness and his power. Every promise he made was fulfilled; every battle he fought was won. Now at the conclusion of the book he asks Israel and us to reaffirm the most important decision of our lives: "Choose for yourselves this day whom you will serve."

1. God has given us the ability to make choices. What are some of the inherent benefits and dangers of making choices?

2. Read Joshua 24:1-13. Why do you think the Lord recounts Israel's history from beginning to end?

3. How would you briefly summarize your own spiritual history?

4. Read Joshua 24:14-33. Joshua and the Israelites repeat the word *serve* thirteen times in verses 14-27. Why is this a good word to describe our duty to God?

5. Why might serving the Lord seem undesirable to the Israelites (v. 15)?

6. Joshua asks Israel to choose whom they will serve (v. 15). What choices do you have about whom to serve?

7. Why doesn't Joshua accept the Israelites' first pledge to serve the Lord (v. 19)?

8. In what ways is serving the Lord difficult for you?

9. What makes serving him worthwhile?

10. What is the purpose of the witnesses mentioned in verses 22 and 27?

11. If you have made a decision to serve the Lord, who or what acts as the witness to that decision?

12. What have you appreciated most about the book of Joshua?

13. In what ways has it challenged you to trust and obey God more fully?

Leader's Notes

Leading a Bible discussion can be an enjoyable and rewarding experience. But it can also be *scary*—especially if you've never done it before. If this is your feeling, you're in good company. When God asked Moses to lead the Israelites out of Egypt, he replied, "O Lord, please send someone else to do it!" (Ex 4:13).

When Solomon became king of Israel, he felt the task was far beyond his abilities. "I am only a little child and do not know how to carry out my duties. . . . Who is able to govern this great people of yours?" (1 Kings 3:7, 9).

When God called Jeremiah to be a prophet, he replied, "Ah, Sovereign LORD, . . . I do not know how to speak; I am only a child" (Jer 1:6).

The list goes on. The apostles were "unschooled, ordinary men" (Acts 4:13). Timothy was young, frail and frightened. Paul's "thorn in the flesh" made him feel weak. But God's response to all of his servants—including you—is essentially the same: "My grace is sufficient for you" (2 Cor 12:9). Relax. God helped these people in spite of their weaknesses, and he can help you in spite of your feelings of inadequacy.

There is another reason why you should feel encouraged. Leading a Bible discussion is not difficult if you follow certain guidelines. You don't need to be an expert on the Bible or a trained teacher. The suggestions listed below should enable you to effectively and enjoyably fulfill your role as leader.

Preparing to Lead
1. Ask God to help you understand and apply the passage to your own life. Unless this happens, you will not be prepared to lead others. Pray too for the various members of the group. Ask God to give you an enjoyable and profitable time together studying his Word.

2. As you begin each study, read and reread the assigned Bible passage to familiarize yourself with what the author is saying. In the case of book studies, you may want to read through the entire book prior to the first study. This will give you a helpful overview of its contents.

3. This study guide is based on the New International Version of the Bible. It will help you and the group if you use this translation as the basis for your study and discussion. Encourage others to use the NIV also, but allow them the freedom to use whatever translation they prefer.

4. Carefully work through each question in the study. Spend time in meditation and reflection as you formulate your answers.

5. Write your answers in the space provided in the study guide. This will help you to express your understanding of the passage clearly.

6. It might help you to have a Bible dictionary handy. Use it to look up any unfamiliar words, names or places. (For additional help on how to study a passage, see chapter five of *Leading Bible Discussions*, IVP.)

7. Once you have finished your own study of the passage, familiarize yourself with the leader's notes for the study you are leading. These are designed to help you in several ways. First, they tell you the purpose the study guide author had in mind while writing the study. Take time to think through how the study questions work together to accomplish that purpose. Second, the notes provide you with additional background information or comments on some of the questions. This information can be useful if people have difficulty understanding or answering a question. Third, the leader's notes can alert you to potential problems you may encounter during the study.

8. If you wish to remind yourself of anything mentioned in the leader's notes, make a note to yourself below that question in the study.

Leading the Study

1. Begin the study on time. Unless you are leading an evangelistic Bible study, open with prayer, asking God to help you to understand and apply the passage.

2. Be sure that everyone in your group has a study guide. Encourage them to prepare beforehand for each discussion by working through the questions in the guide.

3. At the beginning of your first time together, explain that these studies are meant to be discussions not lectures. Encourage the members of the group to participate. However, do not put pressure on those who may be hesitant to speak during the first few sessions.

4. Read the introductory paragraph at the beginning of the discussion. This will orient the group to the passage being studied.

5. Read the passage aloud if you are studying one chapter or less. You may choose to do this yourself, or someone else may read if he or she has been asked to do so prior to the study. Longer passages may occasionally be read in parts at different times during the study. Some studies may cover several chapters. In such cases reading aloud would probably take too much time, so the group members should simply read the assigned passages prior to the study.

6. As you begin to ask the questions in the guide, keep several things in mind. First, the questions are designed to be used just as they are written. If you wish, you may simply read them aloud to the group. Or you may prefer to express them in your own words. However, unnecessary rewording of the questions is not recommended.

Second, the questions are intended to guide the group toward understanding and applying the *main idea* of the passage. The author of the guide has stated his or her view of this central idea in the *purpose* of the study in the leader's notes. You should try to understand how the passage expresses this idea and how the study questions work together to lead the group in that direction.

There may be times when it is appropriate to deviate from the study guide. For example, a question may have already been answered. If so, move on to the next question. Or someone may raise an important question not covered in the guide. Take time to discuss it! The important thing is to use discretion. There may be many routes you can travel to reach the goal of the study. But the easiest route is usually the one the author has suggested.

7. Avoid answering your own questions. If necessary, repeat or rephrase them until they are clearly understood. An eager group quickly becomes passive and silent if they think the leader will do most of the talking.

8. Don't be afraid of silence. People may need time to think about the question before formulating their answers.

9. Don't be content with just one answer. Ask, "What do the rest of you think?" or "Anything else?" until several people have given answers to the question.

10. Acknowledge all contributions. Try to be affirming whenever possible. Never reject an answer. If it is clearly wrong, ask, "Which verse led you to that conclusion?" or again, "What do the rest of you think?"

11. Don't expect every answer to be addressed to you, even though this will probably happen at first. As group members become more at ease, they will begin to truly interact with each other. This is one sign of a healthy discussion.

12. Don't be afraid of controversy. It can be very stimulating. If you don't resolve an issue completely, don't be frustrated. Move on and keep it in mind for later. A subsequent study may solve the problem.

13. Stick to the passage under consideration. It should be the source for answering the questions. Discourage the group from unnecessary cross-referencing. Likewise, stick to the subject and avoid going off on tangents.

14. Periodically summarize what the *group* has said about the passage. This helps to draw together the various ideas mentioned and gives continuity to the study. But don't preach.

15. Conclude your time together with conversational prayer. Be sure to ask God's help to apply those things which you learned in the study.

16. End on time.

Many more suggestions and helps are found in *Leading Bible Discussions* (IVP). Reading and studying through that would be well worth your time.

Components of Small Groups

A healthy small group should do more than study the Bible. There are four components you should consider as you structure your time together.

Nurture. Being a part of a small group should be a nurturing and edifying experience. You should grow in your knowledge and love of God and each other. If we are to properly love God, we must know and keep his commandments (Jn 14:15). That is why Bible study should be a foundational part of your small group. But you can be nurtured by other things as well. You can memorize Scripture, read and discuss a book, or occasionally listen to a tape of a good speaker.

Community. Most people have a need for close friendships. Your small group can be an excellent place to cultivate such relationships. Allow time for informal interaction before and after the study. Have a time of sharing during the meeting. Do fun things together as a group, such as a potluck supper or a picnic. Have someone bring refreshments to the meeting. Be creative!

Worship. A portion of your time together can be spent in worship and prayer. Praise God together for who he is. Thank him for what he has done and is doing in your lives and in the world. Pray for each other's needs. Ask God to help you to apply what you have learned. Sing hymns together.

Mission. Many small groups decide to work together in some form of outreach. This can be a practical way of applying what you have learned. You can host a series of evangelistic discussions for your friends or neighbors. You can visit people at a home for the elderly. Help a widow with cleaning or repair jobs around her home. Such projects can have a transforming influence on your group.

For a detailed discussion of the nature and function of small groups, read *Small Group Leaders' Handbook* or *Good Things Come in Small Groups* (both from IVP).

Study 1. Get Ready to Go. Joshua 1.

Purpose: This passage teaches that although God gave Joshua a big job, he also gave him big promises. Therefore, we can be sure that when God gives us a task, he will also provide the help we need to accomplish it.

Question 1. Every study begins with an "approach" question, which is meant to be asked before the passage is read. These questions are important for several reasons.

First, they help the group to warm up to each other. No matter how well a group may know each other, there is always a stiffness that needs to be overcome before people will begin to talk openly. A good question will break the ice.

Second, approach questions get people thinking along the lines of the topic of the study. Most people will have lots of different things going on in their minds (dinner, an important meeting coming up, how to get the car fixed) that will have nothing to do with the study. A creative question will get their attention and draw them into the discussion.

Third, approach questions can reveal where our thoughts or feelings need to be transformed by Scripture. This is why it is especially important not to read the passage before the approach question is asked. The passage will tend to color the honest reactions people would otherwise give because they are of course supposed to think the way the Bible does. Giving honest responses to various issues before they find out what the Bible says may help them to see where their thoughts or attitudes need to be changed.

Question 3. The Lord mentions his promise of giving Israel the land of Canaan in verses 2-4, 6 and 11. This promise goes all the way back to the covenant God made with Abraham (see Gen 15:7-21). The Lord promises his presence in verses 5 and 9, and gives Joshua assurance of victory in verse 5.

The Lord states that "your territory will extend from the desert to Lebanon, and from the great river, the Euphrates—all the Hittite country—to the Great Sea on the west" (v. 4). Although Joshua conquered much of the land, Israel did not conquer and possess all of it until the time of David and Solomon (1 Kings 4:24).

Question 5. Notice that the command "Be strong and courageous" occurs four times in this chapter (vv. 6, 7, 9, 18).

Question 6. "God's statement, 'I will give' (v. 3) views the land as irrevocably belonging to the nation of Israel; in that sense the promise of the land was unconditional. The appropriation, however, was to be conditioned on obedience" (Paul Enns, *Joshua,* in the Bible Study Commentary [Grand Rapids, Mich.: Zondervan, 1981], p. 22).

Question 7. This question uses the words *prosperous and successful* because they are found in verse 8. This certainly does not mean an accumulation of personal wealth, but rather the achievement of godly goals.

Question 8. Ask the group to silently skim through Number 32:1-27, since reading it aloud may take too much time.

Although these tribes had promised to march with the rest of the Israelites, their promise was made to Moses. Now that Moses was dead, they might have decided there was no need to risk their lives for others and backed out of the promise.

Question 9. Convincing the eastern tribes of Reuben, Gad and the half-tribe of Manasseh to march with the rest of the Israelites was Joshua's first real test as a leader, and he passed it without any opposition. Not only that, but notice how closely the response of these tribes matches God's own words to Joshua. Joshua must have seen this as further confirmation that God was with him.

Study 2. Rahab's Life-Changing Faith. Joshua 2.

Purpose: To see how faith can transform our lives and affect the people around us.

Question 2. If members of your group question why Rahab is honored for lying, you might point out that she was only beginning to be awakened out of pagan darkness. She still needed to be redeemed from a life of lying, just as she needed to be redeemed from a life of prostitution. You might also ask the group what they would have done in her place.

Question 3. Rahab refers both to Israel's crossing of the Red Sea and to their defeat of Sihon and Og, the two kings of the Amorites east of the Jordan. The former account is found in Exodus 14; the latter in Numbers 21:21-35.

Question 4. As a prostitute, Rahab could easily be considered as one of the most sinful citizens of Jericho; yet God allowed her to be the one he used. God had it in his mind to save her and so directed the spies to her house so that she would have the opportunity to respond in faith.

Question 8. Notice how similar verses 17-21 are to the Passover recorded in Exodus 12. Through this event, God brought Rahab into the nation of Israel, just as he had the other Hebrews. The early church viewed verses 17-21 as a parable or illustration of salvation in Christ. Just as the Israelites could only be saved by blood on their doorposts and Rahab by the blood-red cord, so also we can only be saved by the blood of Christ.

Study 3. Crossing the Jordan. Joshua 3:1—5:12.

Purpose: To grasp the importance of remembering and celebrating what God has done for us in the past.

Question 2. When reading narrative literature such as Joshua, it is important to use your imagination.

Question 3. The Israelites were commanded to abstain from sexual intercourse not because it was sinful but because they could become ceremonially unclean (see Lev 15:18).

Ideally, Israel's acts of consecration would be more than just ritual and would include repentance and a change of heart.

Question 4. The consecration of the Israelites was necessary in order to prepare them for the miracle God was about to perform. Consecration was also demanded before some of the other major events of the Bible, such as God's revelation to the people at Sinai (Ex 19:10-15) and the blessing of Jacob (Gen 35:2). Today, many churches ask their members to consecrate themselves before events in which there is an expectation of God's presence, such as a celebration of the Lord's Supper, a healing service or a weekend renewal. Some common means of consecration are prayer, twenty-four-hour prayer vigils, fasting and Bible study.

Question 5. Encourage the group to use their imaginations here as well. Try to picture the priests and the ark a thousand yards ahead as the entire nation marched toward the Jordan River, swollen at flood stage. Imagine the peoples' astonishment and awe as they reached the riverbed and found it dry. Try to feel their excitement when they realized that the Lord was with them and with Joshua just as he had been with Moses!

Question 6. The crossing of the Jordan would have been reminiscent of the crossing of the Red Sea and would have established Joshua as a leader with the authority of Moses.

Question 10. Paul Enns writes, "As a result of the Israelites' obedience to the covenant of Abraham signified in circumcision, God told Joshua that the 'reproach of Egypt' had been rolled away from them (5:9). Two basic thoughts are involved in the phrase 'reproach of Egypt.' (1) God had withheld his covenant blessings from the generation of rebels that died in the desert. (2) The Egyptians derided Israel, suggesting God had taken them into the desert in order to slay them (Ex. 32:12). When the Israelites obeyed the command to be circumcised, God removed from them the reproach of Egypt. The people again stood under the blessing of God, who promised to give them the land as their inheritance. In recognition of this significant event, the place was named Gilgal, meaning 'rolling,' to signify that God rolled away the reproach of Egypt from Israel there" (*Joshua*, p. 48).

Question 11. If members of your group are unfamiliar with the Passover, you may wish to read Exodus 12:1-30 or give a brief summary of it.

Study 4. Jericho Falls. Joshua 5:13—6:27.

Purpose: To demonstrate that the Lord is ultimately responsible for our victories in life.

General note. Some in your group may wonder whether Israel was justified in the complete slaughter of the Canaanites. John Davis provides an excellent summary of the issues involved: "First of all, it should be noted that the destruction of Canaanite cities was based on religious, not political or military considerations (Deut. 7:2-6; 12:2-3; 20:10-18). Secondly, the action taken at Jericho (and also at Ai) was done on the basis of divine command (Deut. 7:2; Josh. 8:2; Ex. 17:14; Deut. 20:16) and thus involves the moral character of God. If we believe that God is holy and without imperfection, it follows that whatever He commands will be just and right. And, thirdly, it was really Jehovah who was destroying these cities and their peoples (Josh. 6:2; 24:8). Israel should merely be regarded as God's instruments of destruction. Fourthly, the reason for this command is clearly stated in Scripture and seems to justify the action taken. For example, Deuteronomy 20:18 makes it clear that this demand was designed to preserve the religious purity of the nation of Israel. The destruction of various Canaanite cities should be regarded as a direct judgement from God because of their iniquity (Gen. 15:16-21, cf. Gen. 19)" (*Conquest and Crisis: Studies in Joshua, Judges and Ruth* [Grand Rapids, Mich.: Baker Book House, 1969], p. 49).

Question 2. In warfare it is common for each side to claim God's support. However, even in the conquest of Canaan the Lord was not on Israel's side but rather invited Israel to be on his side. There is a vast difference between the two!

Question 5. The trumpets carried by the priests were not musical instruments but rather were used to call people to worship and to battle (both senses are evidently meant here). However, the cluster of sevens—seven priests, seven trumpets, seven days and seven marches around the city on the seventh day—emphasizes the religious nature of this conquest.

Likewise, the central place of the ark of the covenant stressed that the Lord himself was conquering the city.

Question 8. The Corinthians were questioning the validity of Paul's ministry because he lacked the typical signs of human power: he was unimpressive in person (v. 10), he was timid rather that bold (v. 1) and he lacked the eloquence of Greek orators (v. 10). However, Paul replies that these things are merely weapons of the world. In contrast, both his battle and his weapons were spiritual and divinely powerful. Like Joshua, Paul trusted in the Lord to fight his battles.

Question 9. When a city was devoted to the Lord, all living things were destroyed and all the city's treasures were brought into the treasury of the Lord's house. For an explanation of why the Lord would destroy everyone in the city, see the general note at the beginning of the leader's notes to this study.

Question 12. The formula for the success of God's people could be summarized in three words: promise, obedience, victory. Encourage the group to see how this formula is illustrated throughout chapter 6.

Study 5. Defeat, Confession and Victory. Joshua 7—8.

Purpose: To consider the seriousness and consequences of sin.

Question 3. In Middle-Eastern culture, tearing one's clothes (v. 6) was a sign of mourning or anguish. Joshua accuses the Lord of failing Israel and jeopardizing his reputation.

Question 4. The Lord silences Joshua's complaint with three words: "Israel has sinned" (v. 11). The sin of one man evidently resulted in the guilt of the entire nation.

Question 7. By confessing his crime, Achan was admitting that he had failed the Israelites, not Jehovah. In confession, we glorify God by acknowledging that he is the one who is correct, that he is the one who is just in making the rules, and that it is our duty to obey what he commands.

Question 8. Another reason for Achan's execution was that the Israelites regarded sin as contagious. Such a disease required radical surgery, much as we would remove a cancerous part of the body. The family may have been included in the punishment because of their complicity in the crime. Certainly Achan could not have hidden the articles in the family tent without their knowledge.

Questions 11-12. Joshua's actions in verses 30-35 were in obedience to the detailed commands Moses gave Israel in Deuteronomy 27—28. You may wish to read these chapters prior to the study for background information.

Study 6. Deceived. Joshua 9.

Purpose: To learn how to avoid being deceived into sin.

Question 2. The Gibeonites and Hivites are referred to synonymously (9:7).

Question 3. The Gibeonites very cleverly omitted saying anything about the crossing of the Jordan or the conquests of Jericho and Ai. These events had happened so recently that a group traveling a long distance would not have heard of them.

Question 6. Rahab, of course, was not commended for lying but for faith. However, she did not lie to the Israelites but to her own people. She risked her life in order to save the spies and to cooperate with God's plan. The Gibeonites lied to Joshua and Israel merely to save their own skins. Their lies caused Israel to disobey God's plan and threatened their spiritual safety.

Question 7. Faith must lead us to action as it did for both Rahab and the Gibeonites. However, that action should not be merely to save our own skins as in the case of someone who believes in Christ merely to escape hell. True faith, like Rahab's, will lead to actions which benefit God's people.

Question 9. "Israel had made the oath in the name of the Lord, and if they had broken the covenant, they would have dishonored the name of the Lord and brought His name into disrepute. To preserve the integrity of the Lord's name, Israel had to keep her word. We know that Israel did right in keeping this covenant, for later in Israel's history, Saul broke this covenant, and put some Gibeonites to death. As a consequence of Saul's action, God judged the nation with a famine (2 Sam. 21:1-2)" (Paul Enns, *Joshua,* p. 81).

Question 10. By serving in the tabernacle, the Gibeonites were forced to do the kind of positive action their faith should have led them to do in the first place. Here they would also be learning about God so that the Israelites would have greater spiritual influence on the Gibeonites than the Gibeonites would have on them.

Study 7. The Lord Fights for Israel. Joshua 10—12.

Purpose: To be reassured that the God who has helped us in the past will be with us in our future battles.

Question 2. Adoni-Zedek's concern is understandable. Israel's advance from Jericho to Ai to Gibeon brought them closer and closer to Jerusalem and effectively cut the land of Canaan in half—a strategic move toward conquering the land. The cities that came together to fight Israel were all in the southern part of the land.

Question 5. Some members of the group may wonder how the sun could "stop" in the sky. Some have pointed out that in order for the sun to stop in the sky, the earth would have had to stop its rotation, which would cause everything else—including the earth's crust—to continue forward in a destructive path. Remind the group that Joshua is not recording a natural phenomenon, but rather a miracle. Surely the God who created the world and set in place the "laws of nature" could also suspend those laws for his purposes.

Verse 13 mentions "the Book of Jashar," which evidently was an early history of Israel's wars (see 2 Sam 1:18).

Question 7. "Calling the Israelite military leaders, Joshua had them place their feet on the necks of the conquered kings (10:24). To the western mind this appears unusual, but to the easterner this was a common military custom. Both Assyrian and Egyptian sculpture portray their kings dominating their enemies by placing their feet on the necks of their enemies. This is also the picture of Messiah at His Second Advent (Ps. 110:1).

"This unusual act had several important points of significance: (1) It was a sign of Israel's complete subjection of the enemy and symbolized the success of the conquest. (2) It was designed to motivate the Israelites to gain further victories over the Canaanites (10:25).

"Joshua followed this act with a word of encouragement to the military leaders that was reminiscent of God's encouragement to Joshua (10:25; cf. 1:7, 9)" (Paul Enns, *Joshua*, p. 87).

Question 10. According to Josephus, who was a first-century A.D. Jewish historian, the forces allied against Israel were 300,000 infantry, 10,000 cavalry and 20,000 war chariots (Paul Enns, *Joshua*, p. 96).

Question 11. Verse 20 says, "For it was the LORD himself who hardened their hearts to wage war against Israel, so that he might destroy them totally, exterminating them without mercy." We must not forget that mercy is not something God owes to a sinful people. If that seems unjust to some members of your group, you might mention that justice is exactly what the Canaanites received—justice in the form of judgment for centuries of sin (see Gen 15:16).

Study 8. Joshua Divides the Land. Joshua 13—19.

Purpose: To explore why Christians often experience so little when we have been promised so much.

Question 3. Forty years before Joshua entered the Promised Land, Moses had tried to lead the people into Canaan. However, due to a pessimistic report by an exploration team, the people rebelled and refused to enter. Only two of those original explorers believed that God could give the people the land.

They were Caleb and Joshua (Num 13). At age eighty- five, Caleb still believes that God can strengthen him to do tasks which seem impossible.

Question 4. This question does not ask the group to read every verse in these chapters, since most of them merely describe how the land was divided among the various tribes.

Encourage the group to explore several possible answers to this question. For example, Exodus and Deuteronomy tell us that God had said the conquest of Canaan would not happen all at once. Yet, this does not fully explain Israel's difficulty. We know that the tribes of Manasseh and Ephraim disobeyed God by not destroying the Canaanites as God had commanded (Deut 20:16-18) but instead allowed them to do forced labor (Josh 16:10; 17:12-13). Caleb's outstanding example also raises the question of whether the other tribes had faith in God's promises. In the remainder of the study, the group will consider other possible reasons for Israel's difficulty.

Questions 8-9. The seven tribes were evidently concerned about whether there would be a fair distribution of the land. Not all of the land was of equal size or value, so they wondered which tribes would get the best and which the worst areas. Because they didn't know what to do, they did nothing at all! Joshua's solution of casting lots assured them that the final decisions would be impartial.

Question 10. Some possible reasons are God's timing or our lack of faith, disobedience and procrastination.

Study 9. The Lord Fulfills His Promises. Joshua 20—21.

Purpose: To see how God fulfilled all of his promises to Israel.

Question 1. The group may have difficulty responding to this question, since many people don't think of their prayers in relation to God's promises. However, let them wrestle with it before moving on to the next question.

Question 2. For further information about the cities of refuge, see Numbers 35:6-28. These cities were located on both sides of the Jordan in the south, in the center of the land and in the north in order to provide easy access to those who needed to flee there (see a Bible map for their location).

The high priest's death (v. 6) may be symbolic of Christ's atoning death. With the high priest's death, the accused was set free from his unintentional sin.

Question 3. The Levites would know and respect the law of God, including the laws about manslaughter.

Question 7. Part of God's purpose may have been pragmatic—not to burden just one tribe with the responsibility of having the Levites in their midst.

However, God's purposes probably went beyond this. The Levites knew God's law and could act as a positive influence throughout Israel as they lived among God's people.

Question 9. At this point in the book, the Lord had given Israel the Promised Land, they had taken possession of it, they had settled in it, and they had rest from all their enemies. The Lord had done everything he had said he would do.

Study 10. Will the Nation Survive? Joshua 22.

Purpose: To learn principles for restoring and maintaining unity in churches and fellowship groups.

Question 2. You may need to remind your group of the things they learned in study 1, questions 8-9.

Question 4. Besides the obvious blessings of wealth, you may want to help your group think of some of the intangible blessings (for example, a sense of accomplishment, the fulfillment of God's promises, and peace).

Question 6. God had established Shiloh as the central worship center to which men from all the tribes were obligated to go for worship three times a year (Ex 23:17). Since sacrifices were forbidden anywhere else, the western tribes viewed the building of an altar as an act of rebellion.

Question 7. Rather than taking time to read Numbers 25 aloud, encourage group members to read it quickly and silently for background information to this question.

The worship of Peor and the sin of Achan were acts of defiance against God's direct command. Both resulted in punishment from God which continued until the guilty persons were executed.

Question 12. Both sides in this dispute were concerned primarily with pleasing God. A tense situation was defused by talking out their viewpoints and the reasons behind their actions. Phinehas acts as a mediator between the two sides. After hearing both sides, the leaders of the community make a decision and report it to the people.

Study 11. Joshua's Farewell. Joshua 23.

Purpose: To remind us of God's faithfulness and to warn us about the dangers of allegiance to the world.

Question 2. Verse 1 mentions that Joshua was "old and well advanced in years." In 24:29 we are told that he was a hundred and ten when he died.

Question 7. Joshua's warnings about pagan nations in the land echo Moses' warnings in Exodus 23:33, 34:12-16 and Deuteronomy 7:16.

Question 10. Israel's prosperity and continuance in the land was conditioned on their obedience to God's covenant with them (see Deut 28:15-68).
Question 11. Someone in your group may question whether these verses teach that God might take salvation away from a person. Jesus taught, "I give them eternal life, and they shall never perish; no one can snatch them out of my hand" (Jn 10:28). Paul also states the promise, "He who began a good work in you will carry it on to completion until the day of Christ Jesus" (Phil 1:6). From verses such as these, we know that once we have been saved, we can never become unsaved. However, this does not mean that Christians are free from all spiritual danger. It also does not mean that those who merely profess Christ without being born again are secure. Perseverance on the part of the believer is the final proof of whether he or she is truly born again. For a more complete study of this subject, you may wish to look up "Eternal Security" or "Perseverance of the Saints" in a book on Christian doctrine.

Study 12. Who Will Serve the Lord? Joshua 24.

Purpose: To reaffirm our commitment to serve the Lord.
Background. This is the second time Joshua has assembled Israel at Shechem to renew the covenant (see 8:30-35). Like Moses, it is also his last official act as Israel's leader (see the book of Deuteronomy).
Question 2. The Lord is reminding Israel that he has been faithful to his part of the covenant. Israel owes him their existence as a nation. It is not uncommon for the authors of Scripture to tell us all God has done for us before asking us to do anything for him (see Rom 1—5; Eph 1—3).
Question 3. This is an important question, but be sure to remind the group to give brief summaries or else there won't be time for other questions. After all, Joshua summarized centuries of history in only four paragraphs!
Question 4. The word *serve* or *servant* is used "as the humble person's description of himself in the presence of his God. It acknowledges the lowly status of the speaker, the total claim of God upon a member of the people he has elected, and a corresponding confidence in commitment to God, who will vindicate His servant" *(The New Bible Dictionary,* ed. J. D. Douglas [Grand Rapids, Mich.: Eerdman's, 1962], s.v. "The Servant of the Lord").
Question 7. The Israelites are confident of their ability to serve the Lord, and say so four times in this chapter (vv. 16, 18, 21, 24). Joshua, however, knows the sinfulness of human nature. The book of Judges and Israel's subsequent history show that Joshua was right.
Questions 10-11. These questions bring up the subject of accountability. You may wish to discuss with your group how you might hold each other

accountable for decisions and commitments you have made during your study of Joshua.

Questions 12-13. Since this is the final study, it is important to spend some time in review. Be sure to leave adequate time for these questions!

Donald E. Baker is the pastor of Christ Community Church (Reformed Church in America) in Palm Springs, Florida. He is a former InterVarsity campus staff member and the author of the LifeGuide Bible Study, Philippians: Jesus Our Joy.